OFF TO THE RACES

Motorcycle Hill Climb

Thomas Kingsley Troupe

45TH PARALLEL PRESS

Published in the United States of America by Cherry Lake Publishing Group
Ann Arbor, Michigan
www.cherrylakepublishing.com

Reading Adviser: Beth Walker Gambro, MS, Ed., Reading Consultant, Yorkville, IL

PHOTOS CREDITS:
©www.shutterstock.com. Cover: © Kutt Niinepuul Dreamstime.com, page 2 ©MalikNalik, page 4 ©Oleg Medvedytskov, page 5 ©Floydsphoto| Dreamstime.com, page 6 ©Ondrej_Novotny_92, page 7 ©Kutt Niinepuul Dreamstime.com, page 8 ©Edward Butler Public Domain, page 9 ©Public Domain, Page 10 ©David Fowler, page 11 ©National Archives/Public Domain, page 12 © Scott James| Dreamstime.com, page 13 ©Renaud Philippe| Dreamstime.com, page 14 ©Ervin Monn, Page 15 ©Kutt Niinepuul Dreamstime.com, page 16-17 ©Kutt Niinepuul Dreamstime.com, page 18 © Ernestos Vitouladitis| Dreamstime.com, page 19 ©Aurassh| Dreamstime.com, page 20 ©Mariel Camacho Cuba, page 21 ©sivVector, page 22 ©Dennis MacDonald, page 23 ©Hillclimb_CCAttribution 2.0 Generic license_©Bengt Nyman, page 24 © Aleksandr Korchagin| Dreamstime.com, page 25 © Andrii Tsynhariuk| Dreamstime.com, page 26 ©Kutt Niinepuul Dreamstime.com, page 27 ©Aleksandr Korchagin| Dreamstime.com, page 28 ©Aurassh| Dreamstime.com, Page 29 ©Dennis MacDonald, page 30 ©Sweetheart29| Dreamstime.com.

Produced for Cherry Lake Publishing by bluedooreducation.com

Copyright © 2026 by Cherry Lake Publishing Group

All rights reserved. No part of this book may be reproduced or utilized in any form or by any means without written permission from the publisher.

45th Parallel Press is an imprint of Cherry Lake Publishing Group.

Library of Congress Cataloging-in-Publication Data has been filed and is available at catalog.loc.gov.
Printed in the United States of America

Note from Publisher: Websites change regularly, and their future contents are outside of our control. Supervise children when conducting any recommended online searches for extended learning opportunities.

ABOUT THE AUTHOR

Thomas Kingsley Troupe is the author of over 300 books for young readers. When he's not writing, he enjoys reading, playing video games, and hunting ghosts as part of the Twin Cities Paranormal Society. Otherwise, he's probably taking a nap or something. TKT lives in Woodbury, MN, with his two sons.

Table of Contents

CHAPTER 1
Introduction 4

CHAPTER 2
Motorcycle Hill Climb History 8

CHAPTER 3
Motorcycle Hill Climb Events 14

CHAPTER 4
Motorcycle Hill Climb Bikes and Gear 20

CHAPTER 5
Hill Climb Racers 26

Did You Know? 30
Find Out More 32
Glossary 32
Index 32

Chapter 1
Introduction

The rider mounts the dirt bike. The motor roars to life. The engine revs. Smoke blasts from the exhaust. The bike rumbles, vibrating its rider. The rider's crew stands by. The rider nods at them. They give the rider a thumbs up. Time to ride! The bike races across the dusty trail. It's headed straight for the steep hill in front of it.

This racer gets lots of speed before zooming up the hill.

The bike's back wheel spins. Dust and dirt fly up in a cloud. The bike is going fast. The engine growls with power. The hill is a monster. Today, the machine will beat it!

Motorcycle hill climb is rough and exciting. Big crowds like to watch. They stand off to the side. Getting too close is risky. They cheer for great attempts.

Hill climb riders love a challenge. They plan their route uphill. They watch the other riders. They know the sport is hazardous. Motorcycle hill climb is fun, but dangerous. They could fall off of their bike. Their bike could land on top of them. A fall downhill might cause injuries. One bad run could be their last.

FUN FACT: Hill climb isn't just for motorcycles! There are automobile and bicycle hill climbs. Runners also do hill climb races.

Motorcycle hill climb is only for the brave. Is the excitement worth the risk? Let's learn more!

Chapter 2
Motorcycle Hill Climb History

Motorcycle hill climbs have a long history. The first motorcycle came in 1884. It was invented by Edward Butler. It had 3 wheels and a small engine. Soon people were adding motors to bicycles. They no longer wanted to use horses to get around. A motor bicycle—or motorcycle—was better.

The first motorcycle was called a yelocycle and had 3 wheels.

People began racing motorcycles on an oval track. They called it board track racing. The wooden track was shaped like a large bowl. It had steep sides. Large crowds came to watch. The motorcycles rode fast. If they didn't, they would crash.

Board track racing was exciting. Cities around the United States built tracks. They wanted to make the tracks steeper and steeper. The steeper the track, the faster the race.

9

Motorcycle hill climbs began in the early 1900s. Manufacturers wanted to show how powerful their motorcycles were. They held hill climbing competitions. Riders raced their motorcycles up steep, paved hills. Crowds gathered to watch. Riders wanted to try steeper hills. Hill climbs became more popular than board track racing.

Some hill climbs made the riders go 2 or more at a time.

Soon, paved hills were not exciting enough. They moved to steeper, unpaved hills. Orange County, California, had a massive hill. It was 500 feet (152 meters) tall. It started with a 50% **grade**, or steepness. It increased to almost 70% near the top.

70 percent grade

45 percent grade

0 percent grade

Hill climb racing in the 1940s

Motorcycle hill climbs were exciting. The hills were a real challenge. Riders were falling off of their bikes. Motorcycles fell down the hill. Few people made it to the top. The sport was dangerous. Even so, the crowds grew. Soon, professional racers wanted to try.

Big motorcycle companies wanted to be the best. The 3 biggest manufacturers started teams. Harley Davidson, Indian, and Excelsior motorcycles looked for the fastest riders.

A 1926 Indian Prince motorcycle

Special motorcycles were built for the sport. They made the bike frames longer. Engines were tuned for power. Chains and spikes were put on the back wheels.

Large rubber paddles have been added to this tire.

In 1931, the American Motorcyclists Association (AMA) began motorcycle hill climb championships. There were separate competitions on each United States coast.

Chapter 3
Motorcycle Hill Climb Events

The rules for motorcycle hill climbs are simple. Riders race by themselves to the top of the hill. They usually get 2 tries. They are timed. The judges keep their best time.

Some hills are almost impossible. Many riders don't make it to the top. They flip over on their bikes. They tumble down the hill. Their bike slides down the hill too. The judges see how far they made it. They look at distance and time for their runs. Whoever goes the furthest and fastest wins.

The motorcycles often take a beating.

Markers are placed along the hill's sides. They have numbers on them. They show how high uphill the riders get. The markers help the judges and riders. Riders can see how much farther they need to go. For some hills, barriers are in place. Barriers keep the bikes from going off course. They also help protect the crowds.

Some hills are dangerously steep. Many have large rocks and natural obstacles in the path. Riders falling off is guaranteed. People working for the competition try to help them. The helpers wear lines attached to trees. They try to catch or stop falling riders.

Riders try to reach a height marker along the track.

Big events happen all over the country. All racers start locally or at the nearest event. Some riders travel around the world to race. Professionals usually race the bigger events. Those pay more and have bigger prizes. New racers can get good experience at the smaller events.

There are steep motorcycle hills all over the world. Local racers get a chance to show their stuff. They can win cash prizes. Then they can try to race nationally.

Sometimes the hills are muddy. This makes the hill climb much tougher.

Chapter 4
Motorcycle Hill Climb Bikes and Gear

Hill climbing bikes must meet **specifications**. Specifications are detailed plans about how to make something. A strong motorcycle is needed to climb hills. Some riders will use their bikes as-is. For others, a stock bike isn't powerful enough. They need better engines. They need to make changes.

Practicing on a steep hill

Modified bikes are allowed in motorcycle hill climb. Modified means changed. People change parts to make bikes better. They extend the back wheel out. They use special tires. Many use special engines. Some motorcycles use **nitrous**. That's a gas that can boost engine power.

standard bike

extended back wheel bike

Sometimes it seems like riders are climbing straight uphill. A steep slope can cause the bike to do a **wheelie**. A wheelie is when the front tire comes up. Doing a wheelie on a hill is not good. It can make the rider fall off. It can make the bike flip over.

This is a dangerous position for the rider.

A swing arm helps keep both wheels down. It's an extension for the motorcycle frame. It holds the back wheel farther away. It makes the bike look longer. It's much harder to do a wheelie with a swing arm. Some riders think it helps. Others think they lose power.

swing arm

Traction is a tire's ability to grip the ground. It is what moves vehicles forward. Spinning tires with no grip, or traction, can't move a bike forward. Some riders add things to the back wheel to increase traction. They may add paddle tires or tires with large rubber spikes.

Hill climb riders have to protect themselves. Safety gear keeps them safe. Most riders wear a riding suit. A leather one-piece suit is recommended. It covers the whole body. Some suits have built-in back, knee, and elbow protection. Extra pads can be added if needed.

goggles
helmet
leather suit
padded gloves
knee and elbow pads
padded boots

Most riders wear a helmet with goggles or a face shield. They shield against dirt and rocks. Motorcycle boots keep toes, ankles, heels, and shins safe. Good gloves protect riders' fingers and knuckles.

Modern helmets are both lightweight and safe.

Chapter 5
Hill Climb Racers

Motorcycle hill climbing is difficult. It takes riders years of practice. They ride up hundreds of hills over and over. They try different types. Good hill climb riders can think fast. They make quick decisions. They know their bike's limitations.

Motorcycle hill climbing is dangerous. A rider needs to know the risks. High speeds and steep hills can be tough. They need to ride with caution.

Good riders will know when to **bail** or jump off. It's not worth injury or death to climb a hill. They can stop their bike and quit if things look bad.

Riders must know when to give up. They can get seriously hurt by the motorcyle.

Motorcycle hill climbing is an exciting and challenging sport. It's hard to believe it's over 100 years old! People love to see powerful bikes race. Watching hill climbs is amazing. Riders want to show who is the best. They love the rush of excitement.

Events and hill climb bikes keep changing. More challenging hills will be found. The motorcycles will improve. More powerful bikes will race to the top.

See if there's a motorcycle hill climb event happening near you. Watch the sport for yourself. Off to the races!

Did You Know?

paddle, spike, or chained tires: used to give the bike better grip on the track

drilled studs: like cleats for tires to help with traction

extended swing arm: allows the rear wheel to pivot vertically and helps prevent wheelies

kill switch: a tether attached to the rider and motorcycle that cuts the engine if the rider falls off

shocks: used to cushion the landing of the bike and rider

Find Out More

BOOKS

Lowell, Barbara. *Off-road Motorcycles*. Mankato, MN: Black Rabbit Books, 2025.

Monnig, Alex. *Motocross Racing*. Minneapolis, MN: Abdo Publishing, 2015.

WEBSITES

Search these online sources with an adult:

Motorcycle Racing | Britannica

Motorcycle Racing | Kiddle

Glossary

bail (BAYL) getting off of a bike as quickly as possible to avoid a crash

grade (GRAYD) a measure of how steep a hill or slope is

modified (MAH-duh-fyde) to change something slightly to improve it

nitrous (NYE-truhs) short for nitrous oxide, a gas used to make engines more powerful

specifications (speh-suh-fuh-KAY-shuhnz) requirements or details to be followed

traction (TRAK-shuhn) the grip of a tire on a road or other surface

wheelie (WEE-lee) when a bike or motorcycle is ridden for a short distance with the front wheel raised off the ground

Index

American Motorcyclists Association (AMA) 13

board track racing 9, 10
Butler, Edward 8

competition(s) 10, 13, 17
crash 9

engine(s) 4, 5, 8, 13, 19, 21, 31

gear 4, 20, 24

safety 24
swing arm 21, 23, 31

treads 23